50 STATES TO CELEBRATE

Celebrating
LOUISIANA

For information about permission to reproduce selections from this book,
write to Permissions, Houghton Mifflin Harcourt Publishing Company,
215 Park Avenue South, New York, New York 10003.

www.hmhco.com

The text of this book is set in Weidemann.
The display type is set in Bernard Gothic.
The illustrations are drawn with pencil and colored digitally.
The maps are pen, ink, and watercolor.

Photograph of magnolia blossom on page 32 © 2015 by Frank Paul/Alamy
Photograph of black bear on page 32 © 2015 by Richard Wear/Design Pics/Corbis
Photograph of brown pelican on page 32 © 2015 by Corbis

Library of Congress Cataloging-in-Publication Data
Kurtz, Jane.
Celebrating Louisiana / written by Jane Kurtz ; illustrated by C. B. Canga.
p. cm. — (Green Light Readers level 3) (50 states to celebrate)
Audience: Grades K–3.
ISBN 978-0-544-51827-8 trade paper
ISBN 978-0-544-51828-5 paper over board
1. Louisiana—Juvenile literature. I. Canga, C. B., illustrator. II. Title.
F369.3.K87 2016
976.3—dc23
2015006747

Manufactured in China
SCP 10 9 8 7 6 5 4 3 2 1
4500573345

50 STATES TO CELEBRATE

Celebrating
LOUISIANA

Written by **Jane Kurtz**
Illustrated by **C. B. Canga**

Green Light Readers
Houghton Mifflin Harcourt
Boston   New York

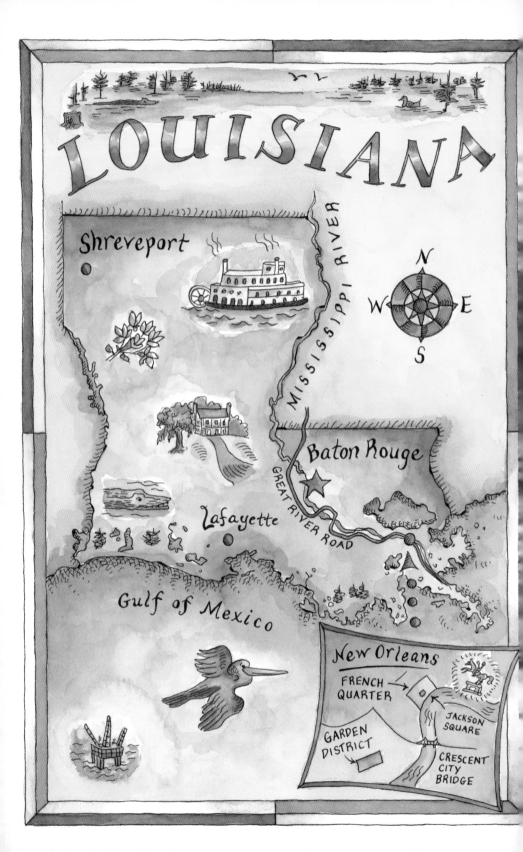

Hi, I'm Mr. Geo.
I'm in the state where
the mighty Mississippi River
ends its long journey south.
The state where jazz music began.
Louisiana.

The Mississippi River starts in Minnesota and flows about 2,350 miles to the **Gulf** of Mexico.

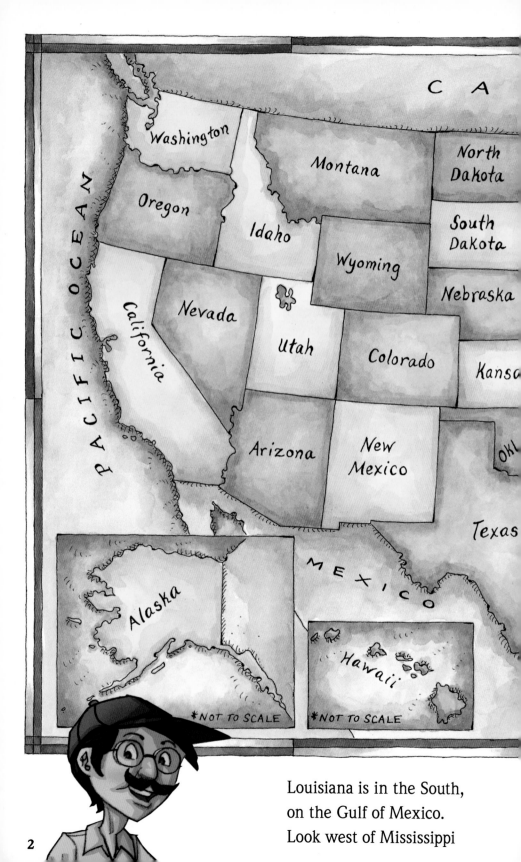

Louisiana is in the South,
on the Gulf of Mexico.
Look west of Mississippi

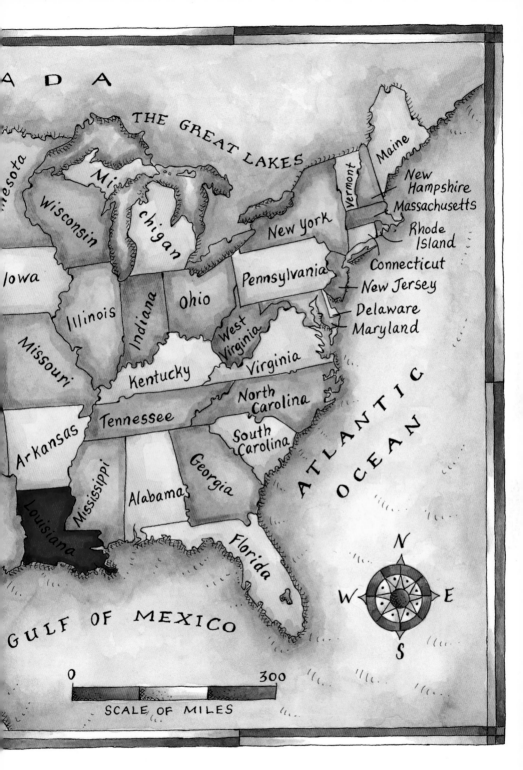

and east of Texas.
Now look south of Arkansas.
There's Louisiana!

3

It's spring in New Orleans.
I'm floating down the avenue
in a giant parade.

Thousands of people celebrate
Mardi Gras here each year.
We all wear purple, green, and gold.
Masks!
Beads!
Catch!

Did you know?

New Orleans is home to the largest
Mardi Gras celebration in the United States.

Welcome to the **French Quarter** of New Orleans.
I'm visiting historic Jackson Square.
It's full of charm and excitement.

Lovely landmarks surround me.

Street performers entertain me.

Talented artists want to paint me!

Is this my best smile?

Jackson Square's major landmarks are the
St. Louis Cathedral, the **Cabildo**, the **Presbytere**,
and a statue of **Andrew Jackson.**

New Orleans is famous for great food and music.
This café is the perfect spot to enjoy both.
Have you ever tried a **beignet**?
You say it like this: ben-YAY.
Yum! They are a sweet treat!
I can tap and snap to the beat while I eat!

Louisiana was ruled by France, then Spain, and then France again before the United States bought the land as part of the **Louisiana Purchase**.

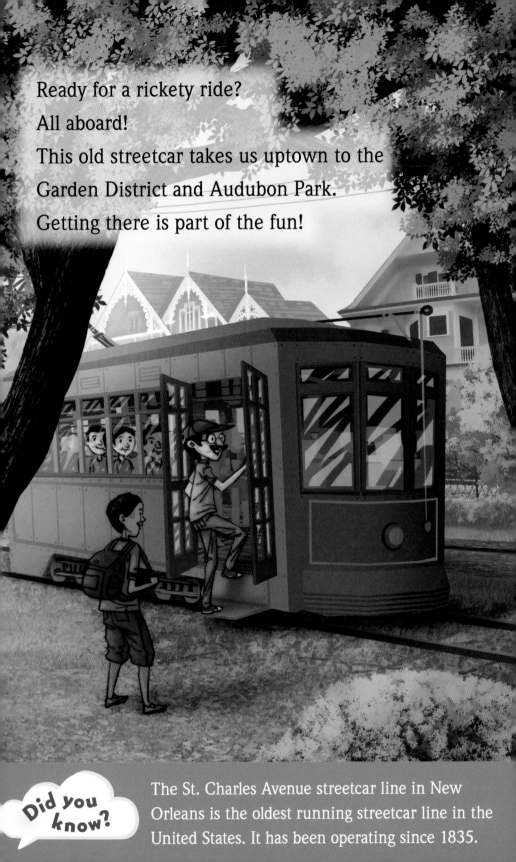

Ready for a rickety ride?
All aboard!
This old streetcar takes us uptown to the
Garden District and Audubon Park.
Getting there is part of the fun!

Did you know?

The St. Charles Avenue streetcar line in New Orleans is the oldest running streetcar line in the United States. It has been operating since 1835.

Our walking tour takes us by
fancy old homes,
fine universities,
and sweet-smelling magnolia blossoms.

Did you know?

John James Audubon, a **naturalist** and famous painter of birds, lived and worked in Louisiana in the 1820s and 1830s.

My favorite stop?
The Louisiana **swamp** exhibit
at the Audubon Zoo.
Time to feed the alligators!

This paddleboat is a perfect way
to see the Mississippi River.
Many rivers flow into the mighty Mississippi.
Many cultures flowed into Louisiana.

Did you know?

Louisiana's early settlers included people of
Native American, French, Spanish, Caribbean,
and African backgrounds.

People's foods and cooking styles mingled.
Songs and rhythms mixed together too.
Jazz music was born.
Let's dance!

Did you know?
Louis "Satchmo" Armstrong was a famous trumpeter, singer, and bandleader. He was born in New Orleans in 1901. He is called the Founding Father of Jazz Music.

Native Americans were Louisiana's first people.
Some lived in villages in forests or on **prairies**.
Some lived in communities on the **bayous**.
Many still do.
My Houma friend invited me onto his shrimp boat.
Heave ho! Let's pull in the nets!

Did you know?

Louisiana's original Native American tribes include Caddo, Choctaw, Chitimacha, Tunica, Natchez, Houma, and Atakapa.

Later, French settlers arrived.
They built cities and rural communities.
Cajun and **Creole** cultures developed.
At Acadian Village I learned to weave.
Does my blanket look cozy?

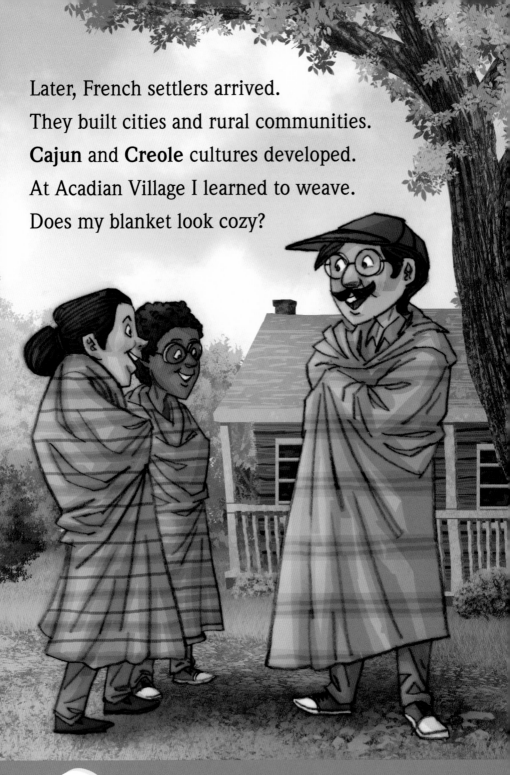

French explorers were the first Europeans to travel down the Mississippi River to the Gulf of Mexico.

Vermilionville Living History Museum helps me learn more about Cajun and Creole life. Today, I'm busy cooking **gumbo** and **jambalaya**. Spicy and delicious!

After dinner we enjoy Zydeco music.

I tried the accordion, but my fingers got confused.

I tried the scrub board,

but I couldn't keep the beat.

Time to try the triangle!

Ting-a-ling-a-ling!

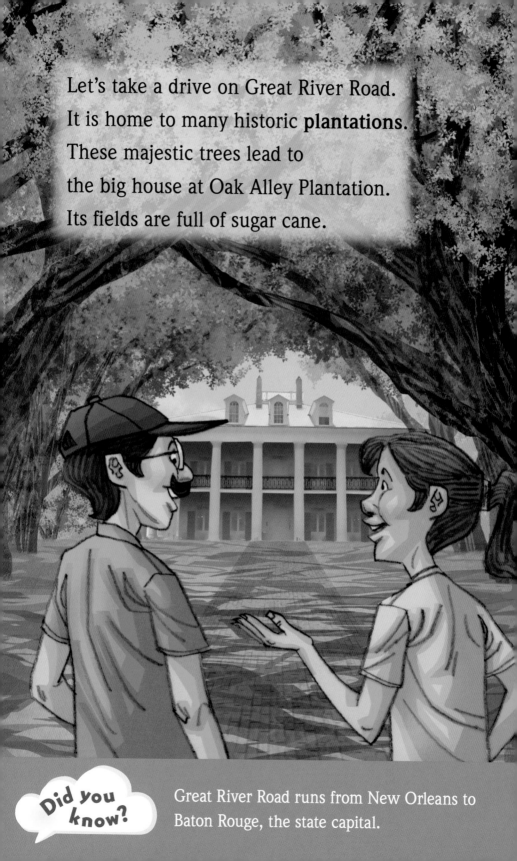

Let's take a drive on Great River Road.
It is home to many historic **plantations**.
These majestic trees lead to
the big house at Oak Alley Plantation.
Its fields are full of sugar cane.

Did you know? Great River Road runs from New Orleans to Baton Rouge, the state capital.

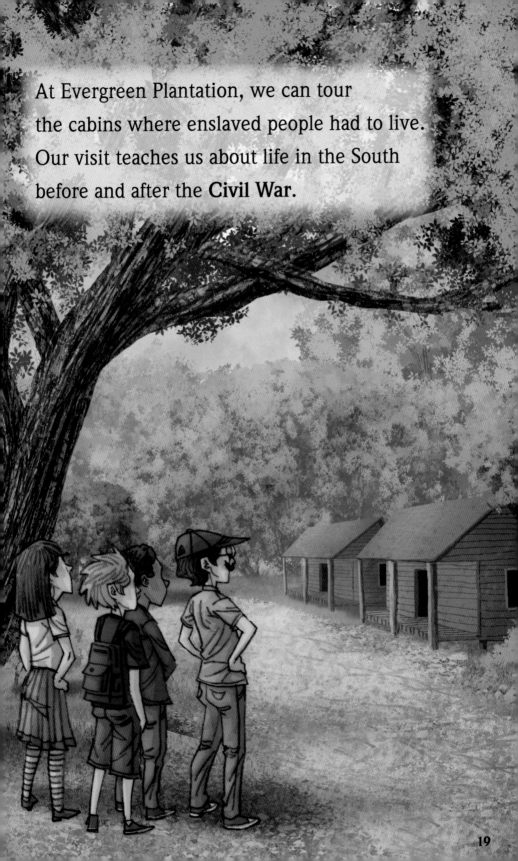

At Evergreen Plantation, we can tour
the cabins where enslaved people had to live.
Our visit teaches us about life in the South
before and after the **Civil War.**

Louisiana is rich in **natural resources**.
Lakes and rivers and streams and wetlands
are full of fish and seafood.
That pelican just caught a big crab.
But I caught a bigger one!

Louisiana is the country's leading producer of crawfish, shrimp, and oysters.

I love exploring Louisiana's **swamps** and **bayous**.
Sometimes they are dark and mysterious.
Other times they are bright and cheerful.
Every time, I see amazing plants and animals.
That turtle sure is spiky! So is the gator!

There are many brown pelicans in Louisiana today, but they were once an endangered species. Conservation programs helped save them.

Louisiana has energy resources too.

Oil and gas lie deep in the Gulf of Mexico.

Workers on huge **oil rigs** use big drills to get it out.

Miles of pipeline carry it to **refineries** on shore.

It looks like a maze to me!

Louisiana's ports are full of ships.
They take tons of **petroleum** products,
grain, wood, and paper to places
around the world each year.

Winters in Louisiana are usually mild.
Summers are wet and warm.
Sometimes in summer,
hurricanes form out in the ocean.
They can bring high winds and floods
to Louisiana shores.

In 2005, Hurricane Katrina caused
much damage to Louisiana.
People have worked hard to
rebuild roads, houses, and schools.
Did I miss a spot?

Welcome to Baton Rouge.
This state capitol is 450 feet high.
It's the tallest of all the state capitols.
I hope there's an elevator!

Shreveport is the third largest Louisiana city.

But peaceful wilderness isn't far away.

I found a great place to bird watch.

Look!

Colorful wood ducks!

Graceful egrets!

Busy woodpeckers!

I've always wanted to see the Superdome.
Fans all over Louisiana whoop and holler
when the Saints play football here.
So do I!

Did you know?

The New Orleans Saints won the Super Bowl
in 2009.

Louisiana basketball fans
celebrate their team's new name.
Go Pelicans!

Louisiana has so much to see and do
and hear and eat!
I want the good times to roll on and on and on.

Fast Facts
About Louisiana

Nickname: The Pelican State

State motto: Union, Justice, and Confidence

State capital: Baton Rouge

Other major cities: New Orleans, Shreveport, Lafayette, Bossier City, Lake Charles, Kenner

Year of statehood: 1812

State mammal: Louisiana black bear   **State bird:** Brown pelican

State flower: Magnolia blossom   **State flag:**

Population: 4.6 million, according to the 2013 U.S. Census

Fun facts: The Superdome in New Orleans has hosted seven Super Bowls, the most of any stadium.

Another fun fact: Lake Pontchartrain lies on the northern border of New Orleans. The causeway that runs from one side of it to the other is the longest bridge over water in the world. It's almost 24 miles long.

Dates in Louisiana History

Pre 1600s: Many Native American groups are living in what is now Louisiana.

1682: French explorer La Salle claims Mississippi River basin for France.

1718: French-Canadian explorer Bienville starts building New Orleans.

1764: France formally transfers Louisiana territory to Spain.

1800: France regains control of Louisiana from Spain.

1803: The United States acquires Louisiana from France as part of the Louisiana Purchase.

1815: The Battle of New Orleans takes place at the end of the War of 1812 between the U.S. and Great Britain.

1861: Louisiana **secedes** from the United States of America and joins the **Confederate States of America** during the **Civil War.**

1865: The Civil War ends; Louisiana soon rejoins the United States.

1901: Oil is first discovered in Louisiana.

1960: **Desegregation** of New Orleans public schools begins.

1975: The Superdome opens.

2005: Hurricane Katrina strikes.

2009: The New Orleans Saints win the Super Bowl.

2010: The largest oil spill in U.S. history occurs in the Gulf of Mexico off the coast of Louisiana.

Activities

1. **LOCATE** the three states that border Louisiana. Which state is to the north? Which one is to the east? Which one is to the west? SAY the name of each state that borders Louisiana out loud.

2. Imagine you are hosting a Louisiana theme party. **DESIGN** an invitation for the party. On the front, draw a picture that represents a Louisiana theme. Inside, write why you chose that idea.

3. **SHARE** two facts you learned about Louisiana with a family member or friend.

4. **PRETEND** you are producing a video about Louisiana. The people who are working on the video with you have lots of questions about the state. Answer the following questions for them correctly and your video will be a hit. Good luck!

   a. **WHERE** is the largest Mardi Gras celebration in the United States held?

   b. **WHAT** body of water lies south of Louisiana?

   c. **WHICH** river starts in Minnesota and ends in Gulf of Mexico?

   d. **WHO** is called the Founding Father of Jazz Music?

5. **UNJUMBLE** these words that have something to do with Louisiana. Write your answers on a separate sheet of paper.

   a. **UOMBG:** (HINT: a Louisiana food)

   b. **WNROB CPANIEL** (HINT: a bird)

   c. **GOAMLIAN** (HINT: a flower blossom)

   d. **RRINAUHCE** (HINT: a type of storm)

   FOR ANSWERS, SEE PAGE 36.

Glossary

bayou (pronounced BI-oo): a creek that flows slowly through a marsh or swamp. (pp. 14 and 21)

beignet (pronounced ben-YAY): a French pastry that is made of fried dough in the shape of a square and sprinkled with powdered sugar; they are eaten fresh and hot. (p. 8)

Cabildo: a historic building in Jackson Square, New Orleans, that was once the headquarters for the city's colonial government; it is also the place where the Louisiana Purchase was finalized; today, it is home to the Louisiana State Museum. (p. 7)

Cajun: descendants of a French-speaking group of Acadians from Canada. (p. 15)

Civil War: the war between the Northern states and the Southern states that helped end slavery in the United States. (p. 19)

Creole: people with a mixed French, Spanish, Caribbean, African and/or Native American background. (p. 15)

desegregation: the ending of the separation of the members of one race from the members of another. (p. 33)

French Quarter: the oldest neighborhood in the city of New Orleans. (p. 6)

gulf: a large area of sea or ocean that is partly enclosed by land. (p. 1)

gumbo: a soup or stew thickened with okra; other gumbo ingredients may include shrimp, chicken, and/or sausage, as well as vegetables. (p. 16)

hurricane: a powerful storm with heavy rains and winds of more than 74 miles per hour. (p. 24)

Jackson, Andrew: the seventh president of the United States; Jackson was also a general who fought in the War of 1812 and won the Battle of New Orleans. (p. 7)

jambalaya: rice cooked with meat, chicken, ham, shrimp, or oysters and seasoned with herbs and spices. (p. 16)

Louisiana Purchase: a territory of the western United States extending from the Mississippi River to the Rocky Mountains between the Gulf of Mexico and the

Canadian border. The United States purchased it from France in 1803 for $1.5 million. (p. 8)

Mardi Gras: a celebration of merry-making that includes carnivals and parades in the days preceding Lent. (p. 5)

naturalist: a person who studies plants and animals. (p. 10)

natural resource: something found in nature that is necesarry or useful to people; water, trees, coal and oil are all natural resources. (p. 20)

oil rig: a structure with machines for drilling oil and gas, usually in the form of a tower. (p. 22)

petroleum: a thick, yellowish-black oil that occurs naturally below the surface of the earth. (p. 23)

plantation: a large farm where crops are grown. (p. 18)

prairie: a wide area of flat or rolling land with tall grass and few trees. (p. 14)

Presbytere: a historic building in Jackson Square, New Orleans; it is next to the St. Louis Cathedral. (p. 7)

refinery: an industrial plant or building for purifying petroleum. (p. 22)

swamp: a soft, wet area of land. (pp. 11 and 21)

Answers to Activities on page 34:

1) Arkansas is to the north, Mississippi is to the east, Texas is to the west;
2) Invitations will vary; 3) Answers will vary; 4a) New Orleans,
4b) Gulf of Mexico, 4c) the Mississippi River, 4d) Louis Armstrong;
5a) GUMBO, 5b) BROWN PELICAN, 5c) MAGNOLIA,
5d) HURRICANE.